The Official Guid

Jessalyn Grace

ISBN: 978-1-7327030-5-6

10 9 8 7 6 5 4 3 2 1

Published by Elevate Pictures

www.elevate-m.com

Hi!

I'm Jessalyn Grace.

I'm an actor, influencer, model, singer, and member of the girl band Run The World. I love singing, drawing, and reading. I hope to inspire people to spread positivity. I rarely post about my life behind the camera, so I'm excited to give you a behind the scenes look!

My birthday is May 25. I'm a Gemini! Geminis are supposed to be curious, communicative, and imaginative. Just like me!

• My Motto •

Treat people the way you = want to be Treated.

How it all began

I never thought I would be able to influence so many people. It was unintentional that my channel found such a big audience. I'd been wanting to have a YouTube Channel for the longest time, but my mom didn't let me for awhile. I'll tell you more about that later!

I've done videos on:
- Fashion and hauls
- Covers of songs
- DIY/Tutorials
- Toy reviews
- My routines

I can't believe I've had millions of views on my YouTube videos! Let's flash back to where it all started.

My first video

Jessa Reacts
to her first video...

My first video was my "All About Me" video. It's still up there on YouTube, if you want to watch it! My voice is so high pitched—really, really high!

I was so energetic, because it was my first video and my first time being on Camera. I couldn't believe I was actually filming a video that would be posted on my own channel. I was just so stoked.

I LOVE being an Influencer!

My mom saw I had potential to be a YouTuber after I did my first video about a toy. I was obsessed, and the company noticed I was filming reviews and invited me to be a brand ambassador.

I appreciate all the opportunities that I've been given, like the singing opportunity with Jam Jr, the clothing line collection with Justice, and now this book! It's actually wild to me how popular I've become. I didn't think that I would reach 1 million followers in such a short time.

After I kind of blew up on YouTube, I realized that a lot of people are influenced by me. So I want to use that influence for good causes and spreading positivity and kindness, too.

♥1

How Jessalyn got started: by her mom

"**I** started a small DIY YouTube video about crafts. It was my way of sharing my hobby, while connecting with others who had the same interest.

"Jessalyn would perk up when I recorded, and then take my phone and record herself. I would think "Oh wow," she really wants to be a YouTuber. I didn't agree to it for a long time, for privacy reasons and the potential for negativity. Then Toys "R" Us held a contest and I decided to enter her. I didn't know she would be one of the top kids from more than a thousand entries.

"They brought her to NYC, along with 19 other kids. They narrowed it down to the top three—and she was one of them. She didn't win first place, but it didn't discourage her. I decided it was time for her to try a channel."

Panda Girl

Panda Girl is really fun, happy, kind, and also a little timid. She's like me!

Panda Girl doesn't like bullying. She doesn't say mean things to people. She wants everyone to be positive and kind to each other. And that's what I want to see in the world.

Like me, my character of Panda Girl has faced struggles.

When she needs help, she'll put on her Panda hat and go into an imaginary world. In the world of Panda Girl, there are pandas that she talks to about all of her problems. The Pandas will help her solve them or figure out a way to cope. The pandas are kind of like parents and guardians—they give you advice and protect you.

When you have a problem, you can pull out your Inner Panda Girl.

One of the times I most needed my Inner Panda Girl was when I was bullied. It was really hard. I'll tell you more about that, soon.

Growing up in California

I've always lived in California. I don't live in Hollywood (but I do get to visit). I live in a pretty small town in the middle of California. There isn't much here, but it's kind of fun. We have almost three malls, one of them is still being built! We also have a great bowling alley, a go kart place, and there are a lot of trampoline places.

Come on over!

I live in a house in a neighborhood with my Mom, Dad, little sister, and little brother.

It's a two-story home that's not very big, but cozy. We hang out a lot in the living room, which is open to the kitchen so the whole family gathers together.

There are a lot of kids in the neighborhood, It's a close-knit neighborhood. We play on the playground in our neighborhood park. Some of them don't even know I'm an influencer.

Meet my dog

Gizmo! Gizmo is a French bulldog. He's beige and his tummy is white. He's sooo cute.

Gizmo is so active. (Just like my little brother Bryce!) Gizmo loves to run around and play chase, so we'll chase him around the house.

He runs really fast, too. Sometimes he forgets to stop so he'll run into a wall. It's so funny.

He knows a couple of tricks: how to sit, stand up, shake, and high five. He loves to play with his toys.

He really likes bacon-flavored treats. Even though he rarely eats his dog food, he's a pretty chunky dog.

He's the best dog in the world!

Gizmo!
My dog

Meet my parents

My mom's name is Kelly. She likes crafts, DIY, and baking. She supervises my social media. She takes all my pictures. Thanks mom! She's a really good photographer.

My dad's name is Thump. He likes to cook, watch basketball, and play basketball. He helps with my videos too. Plus, he's amazing at watching my brother and sister, so my mom can focus on me and get the video done!

Meet my sister and brother

My sister, Abby, is nine. My brother, Bryce, is five.

Abby and I love to play Roblox together. We also like to hang out in her room and talk about random stuff. She tells me spooky stories. I'll tell her about school, and help motivate her.

Bryce is so active that we call him the crazy monster. He loves to run around. Sometimes we watch his favorite show together, PJ Masks.

Abby says I'm...

Smart · Funny · Talented · Creative · Protective · Bossy (sometimes)

My room

I love my bedroom!

Even though it looks big on camera, it isn't. Also, it's pretty messy at the moment.

In general, I love my whole room. It's pink and gold and very, very girly. I really like the style of my bedroom. My mom helped me design it. I told her what I wanted my room to look like, and she literally just did it for me. It came out exactly the way I would want my room to look like. (I so appreciate my mom!)

My Morning Routine

- I get up at 8:00 AM. My dad comes back from dropping off my little sister and he'll wake me up.

- I brush my teeth.

- I wash my face.

- I go downstairs and eat breakfast. My favorite breakfast food is toast with butter on top.

- I'm homeschooled. I do my schoolwork for the rest of the morning.

- The last thing in my morning routine? Getting dressed for the day. Yes, I do school in my pajamas!

My skin care routine

I use the double cleansing method, which is a popular cleansing method in Korea:

- First I use an **oil-based cleanser.**

- Then I use a **water-based cleanser**. It really gets out all the makeup and dirt in your skin.

- Next, I pat on a serum. After it dries, I put on **moisturizer**.

- Or, if I'm going to use a **sleeping mask**, then I won't put on moisturizer.

It's pretty simple but, hey, my skin hasn't broken out. So I guess it's working so far.

You're Important!

Find time
to take
care of

Yourself

Favorite outfits

- **Hoodies** — especially with the thumb holes

- **Cardigans** — my favorite is maroon and very soft

- **Shorts**

- **Flowy peasant shirts**

- **Skirts**

I had my own fashion collection at the Justice stores! It's a dream come true! What would be in your fashion collection?

Getting dressed up!

What makes a good friend

I try to be a good friend by always staying positive and emitting good vibes! I like to make my friends feel welcome by greeting them when we see each other.

I always try to give my friends my undivided attention, and when they need someone to talk to, I try to be there for them.

I also support my friends in what they do! For example, I have friends who are in competitive cheer. Before their competitions, I make sure I wish them good luck and hype them up.

Another thing I do is give my friends gifts. I know I don't have to do this, but sometimes I like to show them my appreciation and gratitude for being good friends to me. I make sure I get them gifts for Christmas and other holidays such as Valentine's Day. I don't ever expect anything in return as long as I am able to see them smile! That is enough for me.

Hanging out with friends

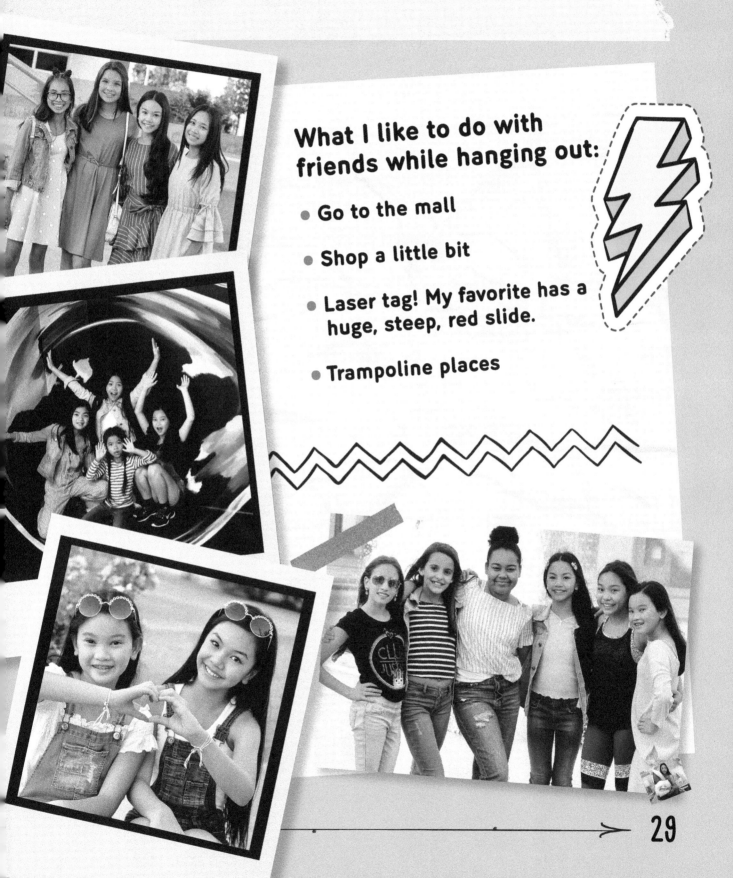

What I like to do with friends while hanging out:

- Go to the mall

- Shop a little bit

- Laser tag! My favorite has a huge, steep, red slide.

- Trampoline places

Ask Jessalyn

Q. Do you have any advice for me to start a YouTube Channel of my own?

A. If my friends wanted to start a YouTube Channel, I would tell them to just start off filming the videos that they like to film and enjoy watching. Film things you like to watch and really enjoy, because it's a lot of work.

When I started my YouTube Channel, it was all for the fun of it. I never focused on being like "okay, I have to keep up with it, or else I'm going to lose subscribers." It's always just been for fun. I can't force myself to film, or else I mess up a lot, or the video doesn't come out feeling very natural.

How to make a video

I just started filming videos on my own. My mom has always been behind the camera, but I've been staying at home more and teaching myself to film them.

Here's how I do it!

1. Plan it out

That comes down to the size of the video I'm making. For my bigger videos, like my morning routines, I'll plan those ahead of time. If I know I'm doing a voice-over, I'll write it out.

But when it comes to my smaller videos, like my hauls, I just film those in the moment and go with the flow. I like to make my hauls a surprise!

2. Get everything ready—including myself

First, I'll get dressed, touch up my makeup a little bit, and do my hair. After that, I'll clean up and prep the room I'm filming in.

How to make a video

2. put memory card in

3. Set up

I now use a tripod and a Canon 80D camera Creator Studio Kit. However, you can start with whatever you have. I started on my mom's phone!

4. Film!

Filming takes me about anywhere from one to three hours, and editing can take me anywhere from two to four hours, depending on how long or what type of video it is.

For some reason, it takes me forever to get the intro down. After I get into the flow of it I'll be fine in the rest of the video. When I was younger, it would just take us forever, because I'd always mess up on the intros.

Power tip: Have someone else in the room to make sure you aren't saying anything repetitive—lots of ands, ums, so's are annoying and take lots of time to edit out.

3. set up camera angle

5. Edit

I edit on a MacBook Air with a memory card to download footage. I edit on iMovie right now, but in the beginning I used Windows Movie Maker. I edit it pretty fast, so sometimes I forget stuff. That's why I'll always have my mom go back in and watch it.

6. Putting in final touches

I add any images and fun effects after the rough cut. If the footage is really dark, I'll lighten it up a little bit, and then if I want to change the color I'll adjust the saturation or the tint.

7. Adding music

Then I put in the music.

The music gets put in last when I'm editing my videos, just because I do so much cutting and pasting throughout the editing process. It's really hard to find music that isn't copyrighted. There are certain sites that post copyright-free music—but sometimes I get copyright notices anyway!

How to make a video

8. Upload to YouTube Studio

After the editing process is done, I export my video and upload it to the YouTube Studio!

9. Create the thumbnail

The thumbnail is the first image you see before you click on the video.

Make sure the thumbnail is awesome! It's the first impression someone has of your video. After we film, we make sure to get a thumbnail. So after we're done filming, my mom, cousin, or I will always try to take a picture of myself in the moment to use for the thumbnail. Sometimes we'll take a screenshot from the footage and use that.

The thumbnail has to be good quality, so that people will be more likely to click it. It's fun to experiment with different thumbnail looks!

10. Add title, description and tags

Tags are really important for getting your video out there. When someone searches the tag, your video will pop

up. Make sure you use the same keywords in the title, description, and tags.

We always make sure to tag everything that's in the video. When we first started out we'd put in things like: "cute room" and "room decor." If it was a Justice haul, we'd always make sure to tag the specific brand, like "Justice" and "kids fashion."

11. Post it unlisted

First, I post my video unlisted so my parents can watch it. Before I upload my videos, I always let my mom go through and watch them to make sure everything is okay and ready to go before officially publishing them online.

12. Launch the video

Q. Do you get nervous when uploading videos?

A. I was kind of nervous at first when starting up my YouTube Channel. Whenever I would film, or whenever my mom would edit and show me, I would get goosebumps because I would realize, "Oh wow, that was actually me! I'm actually doing this!" Now, though, I'm so used to it that whenever I'm filming or whenever I'm uploading a video I can just sort of sit back and go, "I did that!"

I do get excited to upload! A lot of my fans are super excited, and they say things like "oh my gosh I can't believe you finally uploaded!" or "I love your video!" and they'll comment on my other social media platforms. It's super nice to see their comments and feedback.

Music makes me feel...

Music makes me feel relaxed and happy. I tried to teach myself how to play the piano on my keyboard. It's one of those things I want to get back into, if I start having free time.

I love listening to different types of music, like:

- K-pop
- R&B
- Hip Hop

I love singing

Singing makes me feel good. It's my passion.

The songs I love to sing are hit songs I hear on the radio, like pop music. Anything that's catchy to me and trending is always fun to sing.

When I sing, I feel like I'm expressing myself. It's such a surge of energy being on stage in the spotlight.

I had that experience when I was seven years old. I competed in our local fair's singing competition. We went through so many rounds of auditions, and before I knew it I won first place!

That experience made me feel super confident, and I really did feel like a star.

But it didn't last.

The songs I love to sing are hit songs I hear on the radio, like pop music. Anything that is catchy to me and trending is always fun to sing.

When I stopped singing

I was so excited after I won that singing competition! I thought about trying to be a singer.

But in third grade, I stopped singing completely.

A girl I thought was my best friend told me I was not a good singer at all and that I shouldn't even try. She pointed out that she took vocal lessons from a professional and I had never taken lessons. What she told me left a very negative impact on me. It deeply affected me, so much that I lost all confidence in singing. I would only sing when I was alone. I never wanted to sing in public or for anyone to hear me. I thought I was annoying people when I sang.

Eventually, my mom started to notice. She started asking me why I didn't sing anymore around the house or in the car. I would tell her I didn't like it. However, my mom knew something was wrong and kept bugging me about it until finally she got it out of me. We had a long discussion about it and what my mom told me made a lot of sense.

On being bullied

If you're being bullied, here's my mom's advice:

"Pull out your Inner Panda Girl!

"Block all the haters out. In real life, and online. Pretend that you didn't hear what they said. It should go through one ear and out the other!

"You should never let anyone's opinion change what you love to do or who you are."

I took my Mom's advice to heart and...I sing again! I sing even more now than I did before.

If you're being bullied, please remember you're not alone! It happened to me. Talk to a parent or trusted adult!

Advice on being an INFLUENCER

Just be yourself.

Don't worry about the negative comments because they're just haters. They might even be jealous of what you can do and that you have a channel.

Don't worry too much about what other people are going to say about your channel. Film videos that you want to film—whatever YOU want to do.

Oh—and upload consistently! People want to know you're going to post regularly!

The pressure of being on camera

I don't get nervous when it's just my mom and me at home because it's what I'm accustomed to doing. It's how I've been filming for a while on YouTube.

However, I tend to get nervous when it's a bigger production that involves a set crew. There are so many eyes on me and I'm afraid to mess up, since everyone's time is valuable. However, I know I should just try my best. That's the best I can do!

My career

I want to be a news anchor or TV show host. I love being in front of the camera. I'm interested in sharing what's going on in the world. In college, I think Broadcast Journalism would be a good major for me.

I love filming videos—anything that has to do with being in front of the camera while I'm talking would be a perfect career for me.

I'm hoping I get the opportunity to act on a show next. I'd be happy appearing in even just a small role in an episode. I've been to auditions, but never been on a show. So it would be really cool to finally act.

Follow Your Dreams

I Believe in YOU!

Favorite video

I have so much fun in all my videos, but making slime videos are probably my favorite. I love to make slime, and that's how I blew up. After I started doing slime videos, I hit a million followers.

I like making slime because it's a mix of an art project and a science experiment. (We also did a video about the dangers of borax. You have to be careful when making slime!)

Pink slime is my favorite. I also like to do clear slime and put stuff in it like glitter or foam beads.

Do-it-yourself slime

Hi everybody!

See the pastels.

Here's the slime I made.

Add contact lens solution.

Then BOOM!

It's clear and purple.

It's adorable!

My acting dreams

I'm working toward my dreams of becoming an actor! To get started, you have to audition. Here I am memorizing lines.

And, every actor needs good headshots to share...

Check out mine! ●●●●●●●●●●

Live Justice Awards

I got to be a part of the Live Justice Awards in Los Angeles! The awards celebrate the unstoppable power of girls. It recognized and celebrated incredible girls who are making a difference in their local communities and inspiring others to do the same.

I was the emcee for the pink carpet.

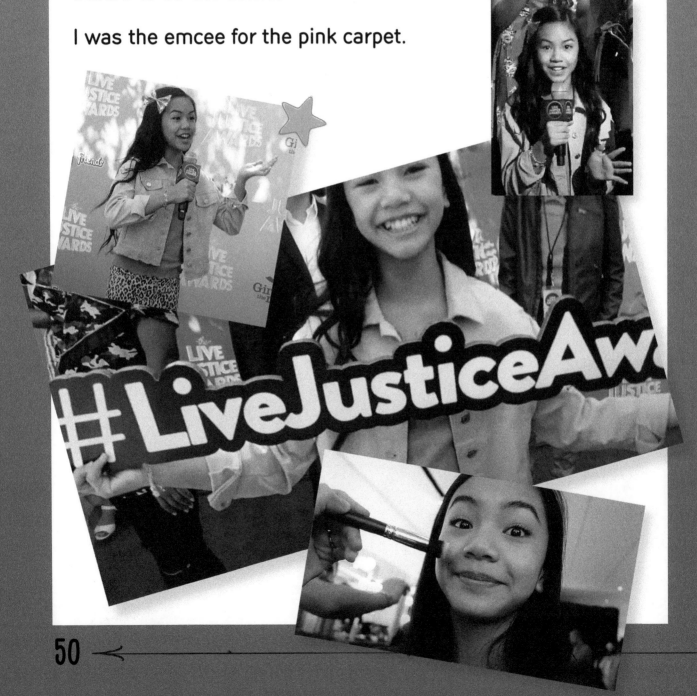

Jessalyn's word search

Search for the words about...ME!

```
A W B F M C U G S I
L C Y J A W P I L N
Y A T K P S X R I F
F D W O L A H L M L
G A C H R R N I E U
I A M B G P Y D O E
Z R V I D E O J A N
M T R P L W R A P C
O T H T T Y Z Q F E
L N W A S I N G E R
```

influencer   fashion   singer   family
actor   panda   video   Gizmo
slime   girl   art

Follow your dreams

Remember how I was bullied into thinking I would never sing again? Well, guess what?

Drum roll, please... I'm in a BAND called RTW aka Run the World! It's a group formed by Columbia Records, Jam Jr., and Justice. My band, RTW, wants to spread positivity everywhere!

My band members are so sweet.

RUN THE WORLD

COURTESY COLUMBIA RECORDS

Our debut song was Rainbow!

We want to share with people that it's okay to cry or feel sad, the rainbow will always find you and help you stay positive and optimistic. If you're ever down, listen to our song Rainbow!

Justice™ JAM JR.

Girl on the MOVE!

54

Being artistic

Art makes me feel free and in control of myself at the same time. I love expressing my creativity with art!

The art supplies I use include:

- Markers
- Colored pencils
- Copic sketch markers
- Calligraphy pens
- An Apple Pencil

Because I love to digital draw, my artwork on my tablet is much different than what I sketch on paper. I can correct any mistakes fast without starting over. I feel like an animator when I draw digitally.

I love drawing

Drawing is one of my favorite things because it's a way I can express myself creatively. I love looking at all my cute creations after I draw them.

I've been drawing since I was about three years old. Ever since I could hold a marker or a pencil, I would draw a ton of pictures. My mom even has a video on Facebook of little me, drawing.

A couple years ago, I started drawing kawaii characters, and that's the art style I've been sticking with ever since then. I really like to draw food or anything that's cute.

Don't worry too much about the rough draft of your drawing! When sketching, don't go into too much detail, save it for the outlining and coloring.

Shadows (shading) should be more cool colors, and highlighting should be warmer colors.

Jessalyn's doodles

I love bullet journaling

Bullet journaling is a fun way to schedule and keep a diary. It's also another way for me to express myself! It keeps me organized, and I find it very therapeutic and fun.

I got into bullet journaling after I found this YouTuber who was super good at it. So I asked my mom if I could start. She bought me my first bullet journal as a present. It was customized and had "Jessalyn" with a unicorn on it.

If you look at it now, I was really bad at bullet journaling. However, once I started practicing more, I got better. I get to be really creative and use washi tape and doodle. It also allowed me to find my love for calligraphy.

January 2020

Monthly

MONDAY	TUESDAY			FRIYAY!	SATURDAY	SUNDAY
		1 New Years	2 Maybe: NewYear Party	3	4	5 declutter
6 Back To School	7	8	9	10	11	12
13	14	15	16	17	18	19
20	21	22	23	24	25	26
27	28	29	30			

Baking

I'm not very good at cooking by myself, but I like to help my mom bake cookies. She makes really good matcha cookies. They're flavored with ground up green tea leaves, so it's in a powder form. Sounds odd, but it tastes amazing. For the first time EVER, she is sharing her secret recipe!

Kelly's Perfect Matcha Cookies

1 stick of butter, soften

½ cup of coconut oil, room temp

2 cups sugar

2½ cups of flour

3 tbs matcha powder

1 cup of cake flour
(Coconut flour may be substituted)

4 eggs

3 teaspoon baking powder

2 pinches of salt

1. Cream together butter, coconut oil, sugar until fluffy and whipped.

2. Slowly add eggs and mix well.

3. Sift in 1 Tbs of matcha powder.

4. In a separate bowl, combine all dry ingredients, flour, baking powder, and salt, along with 2 Tbs of matcha powder.

5. Using a sifter, incorporate the dry ingredients into mixture and mix on low setting. The dough will start to form with a nice green color. Transfer into a bowl, cover and refrigerate for 1 hour before baking. Best if left overnight.

6. To bake, preheat oven to 325° F.

7. Roll out ping pong size ball and place on cookie sheet lined with parchment paper (should fit up to 12 balls). Bake for 15–16 minutes. Store remaining dough in freezer for up to 2 weeks.

Baking

How to draw a panda

Maze

Start

Finish

Work Hard!

Don't take too many shortcuts.

Hard Work Pays Off.

Shhh... My secrets!

Something I've never shared with my fans is...

I'm pretty open with my fans actually. But... I've never shared the fact that I'm a huge superhero fan. HUGE!

I love all the Marvel movies! And DC movies!

I'm a huge fan of the Power Rangers series. I've watched almost all of them. I've seen all the different types of series, from the Basic Four to Samurai. It's pretty wild.

I'm a huge superhero geek.

Super Jessalyn!

If I were a superhero, I'd be SuperJessalyn! This Superhero (me) loves to spread positivity around her!

Even though she doesn't have any superhuman abilities, she's still a hero! She is helping the world become a better, kinder place!

She wants to prove that not all superheroes have super power abilities. They could be ordinary people. People like us, who can make a difference in the world.

Sports

I play and watch sports! I did competition cheer in fourth grade and sixth grade. That's my most favorite type of cheer, because you get to compete against all these other schools and see their teams. You have so much team spirit!

Another sport that I like is basketball. I'm a basketball fan like my dad. Well, he is more than a fan — he is obsessed! Our favorite basketball team is the Los Angeles Lakers.

A FEW OF MY Favorite Things

Food
Korean barbecue! And kimchi

Color
Bluish pink and gold

Scent
#1: Cherry
#2: Vanilla
#3: Pumpkin Spice

Animal
Pandas (of course) and Bunnies

Pizza
Pepperoni with extra cheese. Also, mushrooms, and bell peppers. But NOT sausage or pineapple. YUK!

Movie
BigHero Six

Book
Harry Potter! and UltraSquad!

Susan B. Anthony
She was one of the women who started the women's right movement, and without her help, women might not have the right to vote!

School subject
English! I love to read books and write short stories.

Snack
BBQ Potato Chips

Baby Jessalyn

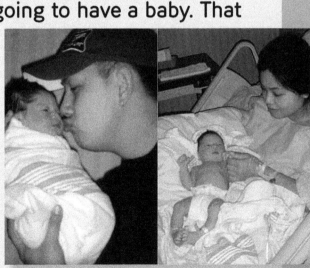

Funny story: It was my mom who chose the name Jessalyn for me. She used to be a teacher for modeling classes, and there was a little girl named Jessalyn in her class.

That Jessalyn went up to my mom and showed her a drawing she did of my mom. Then Jessalyn said, "Look, there's a baby in your stomach."

My mom smiled and said, "I'm not having a baby."

And then, a month or so later, she found out she was pregnant with me. So she named me after the little girl who first knew she was going to have a baby. That baby is me!

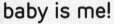

Little Jessalyn

When I was younger, we used to stay with my grandparents all the time. My cousin would also stay there, so we had all of these little adventures.

We were so weird! Our imaginations just went wild. We would pretend that we were pop singers and we would sign autographs and give them to our "fans" (our dolls)!

We would also make up random characters. I don't know how we came up with it, but we made up a really annoying

imaginary person. The person would want to stick with us all day, every single day. So my cousin and I would say, "Hey, can you just stop that?" And then we would try to shoo them away. I don't remember why we did it or what was the purpose of that character. That was kind of weird. Ha! But funny.

My cousin and I are still really, really close. Whenever we're bored, we talk about the random things that we did as kids.

Holidays

My favorite holiday is Christmas. I really like Christmas because we get each other gifts. Our whole entire family gets together and opens our gifts. So it's family bonding time.

One year, my friend DeAnn's family and mine went to Disneyland for Christmas together. Christmas at Disneyland! Amazing! We made so many memories. Although we did have a moment when we went out to get food, but because it was Christmas nothing much was open. So our Christmas dinner was from a 7-Eleven.

Halloween costumes

This past Halloween, I dressed up as Harry Potter for the second time. I didn't know what I wanted to be, and we ran out of time to buy me a new one.

So this year I'm planning ahead! My cousin and I were taking a trip down memory lane, and we remembered how obsessed we were with Power Rangers. We used to watch it all the time at my grandma's house.

When we were younger, we always wanted to dress up as the Power Rangers. So maybe this year we will. She could be the Pink Power Ranger from Power Ranger Samurai. I want to be the Yellow Power Ranger.

Packing for a trip

Would you rather

This or That

Jessalyn's choices in red

Have three feet or three hands?

Be a pop star or a movie star?*

Only be able to whisper or only be able to shout?

Be able to travel in time or to freeze time?

Sneeze cheese or hiccup chocolate?

Wrestle a bear or an alligator?

Be the strongest person in the world or the fastest person in the world?

Spend a week in the woods or one night in a real haunted house?

Have green ears or a purple nose?

Have a tuna fish milkshake or a ravioli smoothie?

*Jessalyn chooses both

Favorite places

I get to go to Los Angeles a lot for work and for fun. I do feel like I've visited every single place in LA. I've been to Koreatown, Universal studios, and Disneyland!

I've only been to New York City once—but I loved it! We got to explore New York. Times Square was pretty cool.

While I was there, I did a segment for Access Hollywood.

Dream vacation

I've never been out of the country, which surprises people because they think I travel everywhere. Asia is the first place I want to visit: **Japan**, **South Korea**, **Laos** or **Thailand**—It would be really, really cool to go to any of them! I would want to visit Japan or South Korea the most.

One of the reasons my Mom and I want to go to Japan is for the food! They have a lot of matcha there—and you know I like my matcha!

If we have the time, I'd love to go to South Korea. That's where all the K-Pop idols live and they have a lot of cool shopping areas. I've read a lot of blogs about South Korea.

I hope to go someday!

This or That

Jessalyn's choices in red

Dog or **cat?**

Crushed ice or ice cubes?

Sneakers or boots?*

Tacos or hamburgers?

Movie popcorn or **movie candy?**

French toast or pancakes?

Wizard or superhero?

Funny or scary?

*Jessalyn says it depends on the weather.

Would you rather

Here or There

Jessalyn's choices in red

Zoo or **aquarium?**

Ferris wheel or a rollercoaster?

Morning or **night?**

Teleporting or **telepathy?**

In the mountains or at the beach?

Where it's hot or **cold?**

In the ocean or a swimming pool?

Eating donuts or cupcakes?

City or **the country?**

Flying or time traveling?

Jessalyn's hair tips

Don't wash your hair every day. That actually can dry out your scalp. Instead, try to wash your hair maybe two or three times a week. If your hair feels oily in between washes, use a dry shampoo at your roots.

Do not straighten your hair while it's still damp! Surprisingly a lot of people do this. It is not good for your hair and can burn the strands.

Do not use a brush to brush your wet hair. Use a wide-tooth comb instead to protect your hair from breakage. Letting your hair air dry is better than using a blow dryer. Anything to avoid excessive heat is good.

Another thing is to find other ways to curl your hair without heat. There are creative techniques where you can wrap strands of your hair in pieces of fabric overnight, so that when you unravel it in the morning it will reveal pretty curls.

What I do when I'm bored

When I feel sad

Sometimes we all feel sad. Times can be tough! It's okay to be sad. Here's what I do when I'm sad:

- I eat my favorite dessert: a lava cake. If there isn't any lava cake, then I'll eat ice cream or any of my favorite snacks.

- I watch a movie or a show with my sister and brother.

- I bullet journal.

- I talk to my parents.

- I draw.

Maze

Oh no! Jessalyn has lost her camera. Help her find it and save her channel!

Start

Nighttime routine

Crossword Puzzle

Find clues to the puzzle in the book.

ACROSS
4. Initials of Jessalyn's band
5. Jessalyn's favorite holiday
9. A favorite animal
13. Her favorite school subject
14. Jessalyn says, "Just be { { { { "
15. Jessalyn's brother's name
18. A sport Jessalyn and her dad likes
19. One of her favorite colors
20. Jessalyn's birthday month

DOWN
1. Jessalyn's drawings
2. One of Jessalyn's favorite stores
3. On Halloween she dressed as Harry { { { {
4. A Run The World song
6. Going with friends to the { { { {
7. Jessalyn is a fan of these
8. What she uses to shoot video
10. Jessalyn's sister's name
11. What Jessalyn practices when she's bored
12. Jessalyn's favorite video subject
16. Jessalyn lives in this U.S. state
17. A country Jessalyn wants to visit

Answers

91

Reading

I love to read books. My favorites are adventure and fantasy. I also like to write short stories!

I don't save any of my stories, though, so sorry I don't have any to share with you. :)

Here I am with author Julia DeVillers, who helped create this book with me. I met her at a book signing for her book series, ULTRASQUAD.

The making of the book

We had a lot of fun making this book! First, we brainstormed ideas. Then I met up with Julia and my manager, Cinda, in Los Angeles to get started on writing the content.

Then, I met up with Julia, and my manager, Cinda Snow, in Los Angeles to get some of the content.

My mom videotaped me telling stories that could go in the book. One of the most fun things is I got to illustrate my book myself!

After the writing and designing was finished, it was amazing to be able to read MY OWN BOOK! I hope you love it, too!

Book credits

Creator and Producer: Julia DeVillers

Producer and Talent Manager: Cinda Snow

Executive Producer: Jeremy Hughes

Producers: Ron Wells, Tiffany Gray, Joe Niedecken

Designer: Cory Maylett

Photography: Robert Kazandjian, David J. Orozco

Cover Design: Quinn DeVillers, Emma Hughes

Special thanks to: Kelly Viriyavon, Tiffany Gray, and Columbia Records

Layout/Designer: Amy Marado

Project Manager: Emma Hughes

Special thanks to Kelly Viriyavon and Columbia Records

And thanks to Jessalyn's featured friends: Run The World, featuring Hayley LeBlanc, Kheris Rogers, and Corinne Joy; Aubrey Woo, Laina Keosaat, Taniah Channita, Mariana Alexis, Alizé Lee, Noe Velazquez, DeAnn Khamchanh, Alivia Phorimavong, and Abby and Bryce.

Elevate
STORY PRESS

Message to fans

Having fans makes me feel so happy. I see each and every one of you as a blessing. My fans keep me motivated. You have my back and you're definitely my support system and a part of my family!

— Jessalyn